CONTENTS

ACKNOWLEDGMENTS 6
ABOUT THE AUTHOR 7
INTRODUCTION 9
LET ALL NATIONS BOW BEFORE ME 11
FOR THOSE LOST IN SIN 14
THE EAGLE'S WING 18
LET ME BE YOUR HIDING PLACE 20
FEEL THE HEARTBEAT OF JESUS 24
DO NOT DENY WHO I AM 26
COME ABIDE IN ME 29
LOOK AT THE LILIES OF THE FIELD 31
JESUS IS A LIGHT FOR THE NATIONS 34
THE GLORY OF THE LORD SURROUNDS YOU 36
DO NOT WORSHIP FALSE GODS 39
JESUS IS A MIGHTY FORTRESS 45
LOVE YOUR CREATOR 51
RINGING OF THE BELLS 53
JESUS IS THE GOOD SHEPHERD 57
KING JESUS WILL REIGN ON THE THRONE 58
ENTER AND WALK THROUGH THE GATE 60
LET THE VEIL DOWN 62
JESUS, VICTORIOUS WARRIOR WAITS FOR YOU ... 64
JESUS IS YOUR HEALING STREAM 67
JESUS MANIFESTS HIS GLORY 68
ADDITIONAL THOUGHTS 70

Dedication

May this book reveal the spirit of the Living God who dwells within each of us who chooses to love, serve, and honor him!

This book is dedicated to the blessed Trinity, Father, Son and Holy Spirit. After much prayer, this book came forth. The spirit of our Lord Jesus spoke to me and revealed many things. This book is a result of my prayer time with my Savior Jesus. I hope it will inspire you to spend time with your beloved Redeemer. He wishes to speak to you and share his heart. If you hear him knocking, let Him in. May the peace of God rest upon you always.

Karen Malloy Stever

United States

Acknowledgments

I thank God, his son, Jesus Christ, and the holy spirit, for all of the love and inspiration they have given me to write this book.

I would also like to thank my daughter, Teresa Penn, for all her hard work typing two of my books late at night and for all her support and love.

I want to thank my daughter, Maryann Stever, for all her love and encouragement along the way.

I wish to thank my very good friend, Teresa Willette, for all her hard work typing and re-typing several of my books and continuous email correspondence with the publishing company. I thank Ms. Willette for all her love, kindness, and support. I love you all dearly.

About the Author

Author, Karen Malloy Stever was born in New York. She graduated from Canton College in upstate New York. Ms. Stever worked at the State Department in Washington D.C. and substitute taught in Virginia schools and in the Department of Defense schools overseas. Ms. Stever lived in Central Europe for several years and served on missionary teams in Africa and Eastern Europe. She also spent time in the Holy Land in 2005. Ms. Stever studied theology with the Bible Institute of Liberty University.

Ms. Stever served as Minister of Music, Choir Director, and Soloist at various churches in Virginia. Currently she is involved in music ministry, outreach mission teams and prayer ministry at a local church in Woodbridge, Virginia.

Ms. Stever has two daughters, Teresa and Maryann and two grandchildren, Korsen and Kaela.

Karen in Jericho

Introduction

God's message has remained the same throughout the centuries. God loves his people in all nations with an unconditional and never ending love. He is forever calling and reaching out for us.

Jesus is the good shepherd, abiding in the field. We are all his sheep. He wishes to gather us in a great herd and guide us on a path of holiness and righteousness. He wants to protect and love us. We need only to repent of our sins and accept the greatest gift the world has ever known. Jesus Christ, our creator, is our savior, redeemer, abba father, and our very best friend. Turn your eyes upon Jesus today and save your soul for the kingdom of God. Heaven and all its blessings await you in the presence of all mighty God and his son, Jesus Christ.

LET ALL NATIONS BOW BEFORE ME

"Let all nations bow before me. I will sit on the throne. My glory will surround all my chosen ones upon earth. I will shout and declare it in the heavens and upon the earth."

"I am the one to adore, worship, glorify. I am the risen lamb of glory. I am the crucified one. I am the one who takes away the sins of the world. I will place a hedge of protection around my holy, anointed ones. I call them children of God. I love each of them dearly. They declare my glory and they are obedient to do my will and the will of the father. To me, Jesus, all glory is given. To me, every knee shall bow. You will see and feel my shekeana glory all around you. My people will know and recognize me. My spirit will rest upon them."

"Know that I am always with you- living and walking among you. I dwell within you. My holy spirit lies upon you. I love you with all of my heart. Call out to me my children. I will hear your voice in your pit of despair, pain and sadness. Declare who I am. I am master, ruler, and creator of the universe. Place your hope and trust in me, my dear precious children. I love you. I adore you. I want what is best for each of you, my children in my flock. You are each my sheep. I am the good shepherd. I watch over you day and night. All is well with your soul."

"Trust in the Lord your God with all of your heart. I will take care of you. I know your needs, your wants, and the desires of your heart. Don't put walls up to separate us, dear children. I want to unlock the key to your heart. I have a plan for your life. Place your love and trust in me, Jesus- not in man. Hold on to me. I am a great treasure to behold. I hold the key to your salvation and I can open the gates of heaven for you. Come and follow me. I have a plan for your life in me, Jesus Christ, the living sacrifice. I will let you soar like an eagle up above the heavens. I call you each by name. Your name is written in the Book of Life. Hear my voice and let me lead you to the father, El Shaddai. He and I are one. We are alpha and omega; the beginning and end of all things."

"Do not put your trust in man but in the things of God. Go forward with the anointing of me, your precious holy savior, Jesus Christ. I have a great plan for your life. Trust in me, your abba father. I know what you need. Many things come at the appointed time. Do not grow weary or give up hope. Place all hope in me, the one who is the crucified rose. I shed all my blood for the sins of the world. The price has been paid. Step forward into my light. I am Jesus, the light of the world. Rest all your troubles and burdens upon me this day, and every day of your life. I will never abandon or forsake you. My holy spirit is forever upon you till the end of all time. I give you all my peace, my joy, and my love this day. I love each of you until the end of time."

Karen in Jericho

For Those Lost in Sin

Jesus says, "Come and take my hand. I want to lead you to a place of holiness and righteousness before my face. I am your creator. Imitate me, your maker. I love you my son, my daughter. I am your abba father. Do not deny my love for you or my greatness throughout the universe. I see all things. I feel all things. I have seen your hurts, fears and suffering. You must surrender all of yourself and all parts of your life to me. I wish to abide in you. I wish for you to bow before my crucified body. I am the glorified lamb that was slain for the sins of the whole world. Come before me and present gifts to me. I am the spirit that wishes to dwell within you. I am the Christ, the son of the living God. I wish to make you a fisher of men. Let me steer the oars of your boat. Relax and enjoy the journey. I am your friend, your abba father. I am joy, love and peace in a world where many times there is no joy, love or peace. Let me be your reason to live each day; not all of the material items or other people. If I would deny you all of the things of this earthly world, would you still love me? Am I your everything? Prove it my son, my daughter! Exalt my holy name in the morning, in the noon time, and in the night time. There is no name holier or greater in all of heaven or earth than my name. It is Jesus Christ, Jehovah, the great I am, Immanuel, the Christ child, Jesus, son of the living God. The father and I are one, alpha and omega, the beginning and end of all things. I giveth life and I taketh away life. I am the lifter of your head, your strong tower. I am the bread of life. I am the sustainer of all life on earth and in heaven."

"A day will come when all living creatures will bow beneath my feet. All who will not exalt my holy name will be denied access into the kingdom of God. Their names will not be written in the book of life. I wish for your name to be written in the book of life. I call you son, daughter. You have chosen and gone down many hidden, wrong paths. It is time to turn to me in your hour of need. Let me, Jesus, be the love of your life. I extend my arms of love, happiness, and friendship to you each and every day of your life. I hope today, you will be found."

"Listen to me, come home to me. Hear my voice! Come follow me. I am the good shepherd. You have been my lost sheep. Let me gather you into my holy and heavenly flock, pure and spotless before the throne of God. I love you. I wish for you to become a great servant of me, the most highly exalted God of heaven and earth. I am the blessed trinity, the father, son, and holy spirit. I have a great plan for your life; a plan to prosper and bless you; a plan to make you happy and holy before my face. Come and learn about me. Know who I am. Come find out what pleases me and what makes me laugh and cry. Come and be a servant of the Lord your God, El

Shaddai. Lead and save many souls for the kingdom of God. I call you by name to lose your life so that I may give you a brand new life in me, Jesus Christ. I am the peace maker of the world. I hold the keys to eternal salvation and everlasting life in my hands. Come let me hold you in the palm of my hand. Let me be a gentle wind passing through you. Let my holy ghost power of love, authority, righteousness, fill you to over flowing!"

"Let my divine mercy, forgiveness, and loving kindness penetrate into the very depths and core of your wounded, bleeding heart. Yes children, I see your wounded, suffering heart. I wish to replace it with a new heart this day filled with all the love of your creator, the father, son, and holy spirit. Bow before me with arms lifted up as you exalt my holy name. Become my good and faithful servant on earth and I will give you the keys to eternal glory (heaven with me) Jesus, your Lord and savior, for all eternity."

"All kingdoms upon earth will crumble beneath my feet. I am planning soon to return to earth in a blazing light, a flame of glory for the whole world to see. I will save and rescue my chosen people, the Israelites. They are bone of my bone and flesh of my flesh. I will establish my kingdom and reign on the throne in holiness and righteousness for all to see. At the appointed time in history the heavens will descend and touch the earth. There will later be a new heaven and a new earth.

My peace will be established here for all. The lion will lie beside the lamb. There will be no more war, tears, disease or bloodshed. All will know my name. All will give me respect, love, adoration, and their worship. All will bow before me. All will see my great glory. I am the light of the world. I am a light for all nations and all peoples of all tongues and tribes. All on earth are my children and I am their abba father. I am the morning star. I am the lamp that will light your path. All roads lead to me, Jesus Christ. I am the way, the truth and the life. All else are false gods. I am the one true God. Those who truly love me and serve me will know my face and feel my heartbeat. I am the vine, my beloved children and you are all my branches. I wish for you to continue to grow, hear my voice and follow me. I wish for you to bare much good fruit and receive blessings and grace from me. Thou shall not have any false gods before you! I am the God of the universe. I am the God that healeth thee. I give all life and I taketh away all life. Come and be a part of who I am. I am a great flame, an all-encompassing fire, a penetrating light of heat, warmth, compassion, peace, and love for the whole world. Come and follow me, the good shepherd. I love you!

The Eagle's Wing

I will soar above the heavens
On eagles wings of delight

No harm shall come to me
My Lord holds me close and tight

He's redeemed the world of unrighteousness
And set the captives free

To soar above the clouds
For all eternity

He offers us a banquet
As we see him face to face

So break the bread and drink the wine
And feel his warm embrace
Grab on to the eagle's wing
And fly to a place unseen

Know that in the end you'll see
The King of Kings, the redeemed

His name is Jesus
Holding power and might

His name speaks peace
With brightness of light!

He will come on eagles wings
In your heart to reign

So don't give up, don't quit, don't fight
Reach high above the sky

Someone's waiting to grab your hand
So embrace your life and fly!

Karen Malloy Stever

Let Me Be Your Hiding Place

"I am the bright morning star. I am the light of glory that will penetrate and saturate the entire universe one day. I will be a blazing light for all to see. This is my shekeana glory. I am that I am. I am the great I am. I am the root of Jesse. I am the root of the fig tree. I am the vine and all my children upon the earth are my branches. I wish for you all to bare good, healthy fruit. Don't turn away from me. I can be an all-consuming fire that will ignite the hearts of all men, women and children."

"Know of me. Learn about who I am. I created you all in my image. Please imitate my goodness, compassion, kindness, peace, love, joy, happiness, mercy, tenderness, and forgiveness. When after waiting for a long period of time there is still much sin and no repentance. My wrath and my fury may come forth and be seen and felt upon the earth. I am that I am I tell you. I will get your attention. In the Old Testament, I am called yahweh, El Shaddai. My son is messiah Jesus, Jeshua. His cousin, John the Baptist, was the one crying out in the wilderness for all people to repent of their sins and be baptized in the name of the father, the son, and the holy spirit. In the book of Acts, I gave you the tongues of fire and my holy spirit. Let my spirit dwell deep inside of you. I long to fellowship with you and be close to your heart. I created you. I love you each dearly."

"You can lean on me and cry on my shoulder. I call you each by name. You are my children. You are a child of God. Let my holy spirit reign within you and be upon you. Let my spirit guide your decisions in life. I want to lead you on a path of righteousness, holiness, and thanks-giving. Exalt and magnify my holy, anointed name. Give me all the honor and adoration that is due me."

"I am your hiding place. Come and follow me. I contain the keys, the pages, the book with the secret recipe of how to attain happiness in this life and be rewarded and lifted up into an everlasting and eternal happiness with me in heaven later for all time and eternity."

"Rest upon me and my words in the Bible. Follow the Ten Commandments. Practice the beatitudes. Pray much and often. I am the God that healeth thee. I want to touch you and heal you. I love you. I call you each by name. I am the holy one, Jesus. Catch sight of me! Grab hold of my hand. I want to pull you up out of the pit of despair, loneliness, depression, and feelings of worthlessness. I want you to soar like an eagle, going high into the clouds. Do not fear or be afraid. Wherever you go, I go with you and before you always. Let me lead you to a higher, better, holier place; to that secret hiding place where only you and I will be. No one else will interfere with all the great plans I have for you. I want you to grow, prosper, and be happy. Today is your day my child, to reach out to the

King of Kings and to grab hold of my hand and soar with me high up into the sky where I abide. Come see my secret hiding place. I want to shower you with many blessings and graces this day. Let this be a day of reconciliation; brother helping brother, families helping other families. Let us all extend the arms of love and friendship to those around us. Let us all become members of the family of God. Time is short on earth. Life will end quickly like a spark in the night. Enjoy life on earth while you can. Soon things will change and be different. Countries will continue to be at war, taken over by others. Starvation, AIDS, war, bloodshed, diseases, earthquakes, tidal waves, and other catastrophes will continue and increase."

"Many thousands of you need to prepare to meet your maker, me, Jesus Christ. I am the only way, truth and life. There is much sin and stain of blood here. I want to wash you and make you clean. I want to give you a pure heart. Repent; repent of your sins and wrong doings. Ask for my mercy before you are all swept away. Come to the foot of the cross and weep. I am waiting for you."

Karen at ruins in Israel

Feel the Heartbeat of Jesus

"I am the gentle breeze that calms the sea. Listen carefully my children and you will get used to the rhythm of my heart. This is the rhythm, the flow of things to follow on your journey through life. Get to know the rhythm of my heartbeat. It is not rushed or hurried. It is even, carefully planned to move and flow in a constant and consistent pattern. I want your rhythm of life to flow in a steady and consistent pattern like this."

"Listen to the sounds of the birds chirping and singing early in the morning. They haven't got a care in the world. They trust in me, abba father, to take care of them and to feed them every day. I am the bread of life. I am the sustainer of all life on planet earth. Come to me when you are weary, tired, and hungry and I will feed you. I am the flesh for the whole world. I died so that each of you might have life more abundantly. Come take my hand and let me lead you on a path of holiness and righteousness before my face. I am the great I am. I am the mighty healer. I am the God that healeth thee. I love you all dearly, my precious children."

"I am the holy one of Israel. I grew up in my beloved village of Nazareth. I died and was crucified in Jerusalem. Pray for me, my children at the wailing western wall. I love you all and I want to capture your heart and your soul. I want to draw all mankind unto myself. Come unto me. I will take care of you. I want to love you, guide you, lead you to a quiet place in my heart. Come into my hiding place and feel my heartbeat. Follow my rhythm and pattern for your life. I want you to receive blessings, graces, honors, rewards, happiness, joy, peace, and love. Come and spend time with me."

DO NOT DENY WHO I AM

"Do not turn away from you creator. Do not deny my great love for you. Do not deny who I am. I am omnipotent, great, glorified, healer, Jehovah, messiah, Jeshua, savior of the world, crucified lamb, star of the morning, abba father, the good shepherd, the glorious anointed one, the Christ Child, the son of the living God, yahweh, the great I am, the root of Jesse, the way, the truth and the life. Do not deny my existence! I am the light of the world. I am the light of the nations. I am the flame that ignites a huge fire in the hearts of all people who will give up their earthly life and follow me."

"Surrender all that you are and all that you have to me, Jesus Christ, the son of the living God. I am the great I am. The father and I are one; alpha and omega; the beginning and end of all things. Let me dwell among you, my people and within you. I love you with an unconditional love, unceasing and never ending."

"Accept the precious gift of my love today. I wish to give you a new life in me, Jesus, your Lord and savior. I want to walk among you and love, guide and protect you each day of your earthly life. I am the good shepherd. You are all my beloved sheep. Stay close together in my flock. Let me gather you all across the earth in one very large group. I will surround you all with beautiful ringing bells."

"This will declare my glory, my majesty, and my omnipotence among all mankind on planet earth. I want to save you all for the kingdom of God. I am the lamp beneath your feet. I will give you heat, warmth, comfort, compassion, peace, joy, and love overflowing. Come all you sheep and gather into my herd, my flock. Time is short. Come and join the family of God, me, Jesus Christ before it is too late. Satan wants you to burn in the flames of hell. Say 'No' to Satan's evil ways and sins and say 'Yes' to me, your savior, Jesus."

Mount of Olives, Jerusalem

Come Abide in Me

"Come and grab hold of the light. It is my everlasting love and affection that I wish to give each of you, my children. I love you. I call out to you in a dark and sinful world. Do not deny my great overwhelming love I have for each of you my precious children. Come receive me and my love. I want to pull you into the light of my presence. Come and live within my heart and let me dwell inside your heart. I am the King of Kings and Lord of Lords. Let my light shine forth from you this day."

"I wish to send you out to the peoples of the world as a beacon of hope, light, love, joy and peace. I wish for you all to be bright, glowing, shining lights of peace in a world where there is much hatred, bloodshed, violence, war, sister against sister, and brother against brother. Make a difference in this world that you live in. Introduce people and children to the living God, me, Jesus Christ. I live and walk among all of you each day."

"I see your trials, struggles, tribulations, hurts, pains, abuse, and neglect problems. I want to help you, love you and comfort you. I want to fill you with my abiding peace and joy. Come unto me. I am waiting to give you my mercy, my compassion, my forgiveness, my loving kindness. I love you, my children.

So many of you are from dysfunctional families. I wish to be your father, your mother, your very best friend; all of you who are tired, lonely, depressed, and sick. Come unto me and I will give you rest. I stretch out my arms of love, warmth, heat, and strength to you this day. I wish to be your companion. Talk to me, pray to me. I am your abba father. I am the light of the world. I am the peacemaker of the world. Come to me in your times of great troubles, distress and sickness. I am the lifter of your head. I will carry you through the storms and gently place you on solid ground. I am your savior, messiah. Come abide in me."

Look at the Lilies of the Field

"My dear children let not your hearts be troubled. I love you all dearly with a fatherly love. I am the king of glory and I will manifest that glory throughout the heavens and the whole earth. Come and taste me and the universe I have created. Come and explore the things of the earth (nature). Enjoy all of the animals, flowers, birds, cultures, and races of people, beaches for swimming, boating, fishing, beautiful mountains, horseback riding, ice-skating, skiing, painting, sculpturing, and wonderful music to play and sing. I have provided many sports for you to enjoy upon the earth."

"All I ask dear children is that you love, honor, and serve me. Look at the beautiful lilies of the field. Could you not pray there and honor and exalt my name? Could you possibly build a little chapel there to stop and pray to me, sing, light a candle, and talk to me and tell me your problems? I want you to have everything wonderful in life. Ask and it shall be given to you in due time my children."

"Come and abide in me. I am the good shepherd and you are all my sheep. I care about each one of you. Don't be afraid to talk to me and call out my name. I will hear you. I will speak to you and guide you. I love you. Come unto me and I will give you rest. I want to give you all the treasures of the earth."

"Hold onto me! Grab my hand! I am a never ending Godhead. I always was and always shall be. I am that I am. I am the God that healeth thee! Don't give up! Run to me in your times of sorrow, pain and troubles. I'm waiting for you to call out to me. I love you. Don't hide and run away from me. I am your one true God. Know of me. Find out who I am. I am your life line to all eternity in heaven. I am Jesus Christ, your Lord and savior."

Petra, Jordan

Jesus is a Light for the Nations

Jesus is a full, glorified light that saturates and penetrates the entire heavens, universe, and whole earth. His love is manifested in this glorious, magnificent light of glory. It stretches beyond all limits and boundaries. It has no exact dimension; it is all knowing and everywhere. It is all existence and all knowledge. It is hard to describe in a human language. It is far above the dimensions, comprehension, and vocabulary of planet earth. It is full of a tremendous energy and power beyond anything you would ever recognize on planet earth. It is an all-encompassing flame of energized, burning light.

Jesus is an all-consuming light, energy source, and porthole to human life and energy source for all life. Jesus is a mighty strong pillar of light for all the nations. Look upward to this pillar of light and strength, Jesus Christ, to help with all of your country's problems, catastrophes, and worries.

Jesus, the light of the world, is the answer, not all your material items and money. "Place your trust, faith, and your very life in your Maker and creator, me, the light of the world, Jesus Christ. I love each of you and adore you with the sweet, tender love a father has for his precious children. Come and bow before me. Offer me the gift of your time, presence, prayers, devotion and adoration of who I am. I want to be your everything."

The Glory of the Lord Surrounds You

The glory of the Lord is all around you. Praise be to God! Praise be his holy, anointed name! He is an everlasting Godhead, ordained before all time. He was and always will be the living stone to stand on, the rock of salvation to cling to; our strong tower to lean on. Halleluiah to the risen Lord, our redeemer!

Jesus is your refuge and your hiding place. All you people of many nations in despair, financial trouble with much fighting and bloodshed, seek the Lord's face. His name is Jesus Christ. He loves you with all of his heart. He is an everlasting God, father, son and holy spirit. He wishes to cover you with a blanket of protection, love, mercy, peace, and forgiveness. He is your friend and he cares deeply about you. Come before the feet of Jesus on the cross. He wants to lift your burdens and give you comfort, compassion, peace, joy, and happiness.

Jesus loves each of you as his children. He is forever calling out to you. He wishes to take your hand and lead you home to the Father, yahweh, and himself, Jesus Christ. He wants to fill you with his holy spirit. He wants to reign as Lord and King of your life this day. To God be all glory, praise and honor. For thine is the kingdom, power and glory forever and ever. Amen.

He seeks to save a world of people and nations that are lost. They pray to no God at all or they worship many false gods. Jesus Christ wants to capture and save your soul for the kingdom of God. Let all thy kingdoms fall, those that do not give all honor, praise and glory to him alone. Jesus is the risen Lord, the messiah. Jesus is the savior of the world. Put all your faith and trust in this redeemer who died for all your sins and the sins of all humanity. He is forever seeking you out, calling you by name. He wants to communicate with you. He is the good shepherd and you are all his sheep. He wants to gather you who are his flock and place you under his spiritual blanket of protection. He wishes to kiss and heal your wounds. He is the master healer. He has answers and solutions to your problems. He extends his loving arms to all of you. Jesus wishes for you each to step into the light of his heavenly presence. His spirit abides in this powerful, holy, anointed light. Grab hold of Jesus' might, power, majesty, omnipotence in this light of glory. This light is for the whole world. It is a powerful light of grace, love, and peace for all nations of the world. Jesus is at the core of this light. Stretch out your hand toward Jesus and step into the light of his glorious presence. He is waiting to change your heart, your attitude, and the direction of your life. He wants you to become a child of the King of Kings and Lord of Lords. He is the great I am.

Be prepared for the day of his coming amongst the nations. He is coming soon in a blazing light of glory, fire, heat, energy, and power. All will see and know his mighty omnipotence. His shekeana glory and majesty will cover the heavens and the earth. He wishes for all of you to love, honor and serve him for who he is. He is your first and last breath. He is your abba father, your best friend. He is your creator, messiah, lamb of glory, savior, redeemer, sword and word of truth. He is life itself. He is all eternity enveloped in a huge, colorful blanket of peace, joy, love, and happiness.

Run to your creator, Jesus Christ, and grab hold of his hand. Let Jesus lead you on a path of pure peace and love filled with much grace. He wishes to fill you to overflowing with his mercy, loving kindness, compassion, and blessings. Hurry, now is the time to call upon your Lord, savior, and master. His name is Jesus Christ. He wishes to surround you all in his shekeana glory!

DO NOT WORSHIP FALSE GODS

"The sun will not shine one day. The moon will be hidden. You will not see the stars. I am all mighty God. I will not shed my grace on you!

I will not ignore all these false gods that many of you worship. I will crush them under my feet. My feet had the nails driven into them. I was the one who was crucified on the wooden cross for the sins of the whole world. I am the crucified lamb that shed all of my blood."

"I will not face a false god. I am the only face of a true God in the universe. I will split every temple, shrine, church and mosque that has people praying and worshiping a false god. I am Jehovah, the great I am. I will have no false gods before me. I am the King of Kings and the Lord of Lords. Do not put your trust and faith in other gods. They are all false. I am the resurrection. I am the resurrected one, the holy and anointed one. I am Jesus Christ and I am alive! I watch and see all things upon the earth. You cannot hide your face or your actions from me. I am omnipotent, all-powerful and all-knowing. I will crush you with a huge catastrophe whenever I wish to get your attention."

"You should be aware of the strong winds of a cyclone, hurricane, and heavy rains. Be careful of avalanches, mudslides, bad lightning storms and deadly high magnitude earthquakes. I control all the weather patterns upon the earth. Watch out for active volcanoes and deadly diseases. Your life remains always in the palm of my hand. Do not take my power, wrath and fury lightly! I am the great I am. I decide when each human life begins and ends. All will be for the glory of me, Jesus Christ, or it will cease to exist. It will be crushed beneath my feet. I will no longer put up with all these false gods upon the earth. My tolerance has run out. Many religions are the root of much evil and slavery and bondage system. It causes much harm to human beings. It strips them of many human freedoms and rights."

"Know that I am coming when you least expect it. I am the one who can calm the seas or make them roar! I am the one who can make the earth safe beneath your feet or split it wide open and devour you. I beg you all on earth to bow before my feet and praise and adore my holy name. I am the bread of life! I came in the flesh long ago to set the captives free. I am yahweh, El Shaddai, messiah, the Christ Child, the everlasting redeemer of planet earth. I am Jesus, your best friend. I am the rock you need to stand on. I am the living stone of your life. Place your future in my hands. I commended my spirit to the father just before I died on the cross. You need to commend your spirit to me, Jesus. You do not know the minute you will take your last breath and die. I wish for your soul to be saved for the kingdom of God. Bow down and serve your master.

I, Jesus Christ, created the universe. I am Jehovah Jirah and Jehovah Nissi. Place all your trust in me."

"I love you my children. I freely give each of you all my love. If only you would take it and follow me. I am the good shepherd. You are all my sheep. Many of you are lost and in sin and worshipping false gods. Come take hold of my hand. Let me pray for you. I want to save you from yourself and from wrong choices."

"Satan delights in devouring you unto himself. He wishes for all of you to burn in the flames of hell for eternity! He wants your soul to burn in the fires of hell forever! I, Jesus, wish for your soul to be saved for the kingdom of heaven. I love you. Please imitate me and my goodness, mercy, and loving kindness towards others. I am forever calling out your names. Listen for my voice. It is a voice calling out in the wilderness. I wish to lead you on a path of holiness before my face. I repeat, come to the foot of the cross. There you will receive my mercy, forgiveness, compassion and loving kindness. I love you my children. Let your life center on the cross and on the blood I shed for you. You are all my beloved children from many nations and tribes, tongues, and races. Come to me and I will give you rest. All who love and serve me will be filled with the holy light of my presence. They will receive much grace, peace, love, and happiness. Please hurry and follow the light of my love. Listen for the rhythm of my heartbeat. I want to set you on a path of righteousness and holiness before my face. I knew your name before you were born. I call out your name today. Come follow me, the good shepherd. I want to set all the captives free. I am your hiding place; not all of the false gods, statues, and temples you have built."

"May each of you accept my love, peace, and mercy or you may receive wrath, fury, and great anger in days and months to come. The choice is yours my dear children. I beg you to come and follow your Lord and savior, me, Jesus Christ. Then, your soul shall be saved for the kingdom of God. Otherwise, a bad fate may await you. Do not place your trust, faith, and love in a false god. I, Jesus Christ, am the way, truth and the life. He who knows and loves me, knows and loves the father. I am the one true vine and you my children are all the branches. Learn of me by reading the Bible and going to church. Love me with all of your heart and love your neighbor as yourself. Make me, Jesus, an instrument of your peace. Do all things and bare good fruits for the kingdom of God. I love you all. Hurry to me, Jesus Christ."

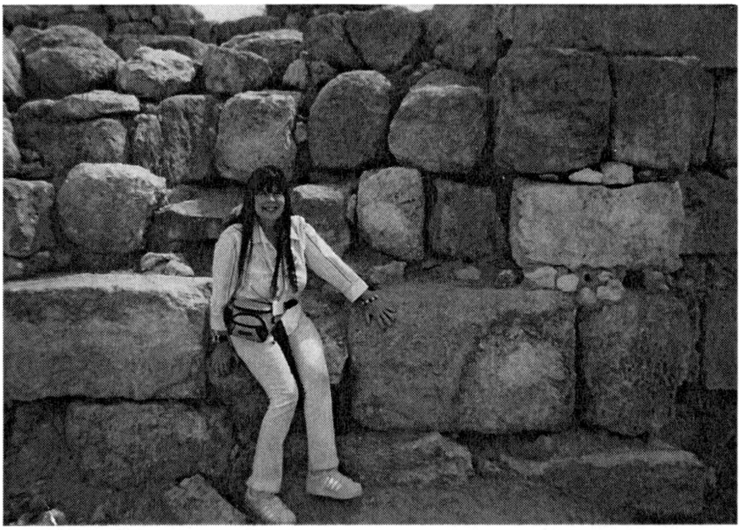

Author, Karen Stever, in Petra, Jordan

Jesus is a Mighty Fortress

"Let the whole earth declare my awesome glory. I am King Jehovah, over heaven and earth. I am the way, the truth and the life. No one will go to the father until they bow before me, his only begotten son. King Jesus is my name. "

"Behold my face in the clouds my precious children. I call you each by name. I invite you to be a part of my kingdom. I am the great and mighty deliverer. I am the conquering, victorious warrior. I am the one who will set all the captives free. Weep before the foot of the cross and you will feel my great love for you. Confess your sins and ask for my great mercy and loving kindness today."

"I am a mighty fortress. The heavens will declare my great glory. It stretches from here to eternity. It has no limits and no boundaries. I cannot be contained. I am like a huge, overwhelming flame that spreads and gets larger and larger. Before you know it, the whole planet will be lit by my flame. Let your light shine for me, your savior, your king. Come and worship me, Jesus, on bended knee. Come and comfort me, spend time with me. I love each of you very much. You are each a special treasure that I created. Call upon my name in your pain, sorrow and confusion. I will lead you on a path of holiness. I will place you in the direction that will lead you to my sacred heart. Let our hearts beat as one. I am your abba father. I love you my children. I will take care of you. "

"Place your life in my hands. Let my spirit rise within you to overflowing. Speak forth in great tongues of fire. Know that I am a lamp unto your feet. Do not look to man to lead and guide you, or to solve your problems. Look to me, your Lord and your God, to lead you on the path of righteousness. I am the one who died for you. I paid the price for all your sins. Do not be sad! Do not cry! I will never abandon you. I am always with you my dear children until the end of time. I will never leave or forsake you. I chose you before you were born to be my very own. Come unto me, and I will call you blessed. I want you to share in the holy life of the kingdom of God. Offer yourself as a sacrifice to the King of Kings and Lord of Lords. Glory to God in the highest! I want to place and bring peace, love, joy, and comfort into the hearts of my chosen beloved ones. Come and place all your trust, faith, and love in me, your messiah, lord and savior today. Let me set you free. Let me erase all tears from your eyes. I am the holy, anointed one. Do not wander out in the field alone and lost. Follow me. I am your husband, your spouse, your very best friend! You are not alone. I walk beside you. I walk in front of you and behind you. I call you my beloved sons and daughters of the most-high God."

"Have no other gods before you. All else are false. I love

you! I love you! Do not deny my deity. I am the God to worship on planet earth. All other gods and animals are false. I am the one to heal you, to set you free, and to give you gifts of the holy spirit! Call upon my name, Jesus Christ, and I will move heaven and earth for you. I will scatter the enemies away from you. I will place a veil and a shield of protection around you. You are mine! You belong to me! I adore you and love you so very much. I see my devoted children and how much you pray to me, sing praises to my mighty name, how you study my word, and how you preach and teach my word to others, it brings tears, jubilation, and joy to my face. Some of you, my children, love me beyond all measure and beyond all words! Even speaking in tongues cannot express how much you love me, King Jesus. I am your everything and that pleases me beyond measure. I have already prepared a beautiful crown of glory for you up in heaven and a very nice, beautiful mansion for you to live in. Do not look for wealth and material items on planet earth. All can be gone, disappear, or be destroyed in the twinkle of an eye. Look upwards towards heaven for your lasting treasures my children. I suspect that you, my chosen ones, will sit to the right of me, King Jesus, up in heaven and also when I establish my kingdom and reign upon the earth for a thousand years. I love you, my sweet, adorable children. Do not harden your hearts with troubles. Look to me, your abba father, to love and take care of you and to bring peace and comfort to you."

"Time is precious and plentiful in heaven. It lasts for all eternity. It is limitless, a treasure that never runs out. It goes on forever. Spend this time, this limitless treasure with me, your savior, Jesus Christ. I am the one that created you. Come and worship and adore me, your God, and you will feel better. I will fill you to over flowing with my immense holy spirit filled with much love, power, and authority! Reach out to me in your dark despair. I am never far away from you my children. Focus on me, the sparrow. Call upon my name and I will open the gates of heaven to you, my beloved children. I will dispatch thousands of angels to you. Whatever you need, I will give it to you. Just ask, and you will receive."

"Come into the secret place of my heart and abide with me there. Hear my voice calling out to you in the wind, rain, and flames of my fire. I burn for you. I am the lamp that is lit beneath your feet. Step toward the flame of my heart, warmth today, and receive my over flowing love for you. I care about you. I made you in my image. Lean on me for direction and understanding. I am your strong tower. Catch sight of me. I am the all-powerful, omnipotent one. Come and see and feel my shekeana glory upon you this day. I am a mighty fortress and I will conquer all my enemies from the four corners of the earth. I will be the one to set the captives free. I will release my spirit of truth upon the whole earth and will see my great glory."

"I will come in a great blazing and penetrating light for the whole world to witness. I will light up the darkness. The trumpets will continue to blow throughout the four corners of the earth. Many catastrophes such as, hurricanes, tornadoes, earthquakes, typhoons, tidal waves, aids, diseases, starvation, wars and bloodshed will continue and intensify. I am cleansing and purifying planet earth before I return to conquer and save what is mine, Israel. "

"Ephesians 6:10-18 (NIV) Finally be strong in the Lord and in his mighty power. Put on the full armor of God so that you can take your stand against the devil's schemes. For our struggles are not against flesh and blood but against the rules, authorities and powers of this dark world and against the spiritual forces of evil in the heavenly realms. Therefore, put on the full armor of God, so that when the day of evil comes, you may be able to stand your ground and after you have done everything to stand, stand firm then with the belt of truth buckled around your waist, with the breastplate of righteousness in place, and with your feet fitted with the readiness that comes from the gospel of peace. In addition to this, take up the shield of faith with which you can extinguish all the flaming arrows of the evil one. Take the helmet of salvation and the sword of the spirit which is the word of God. And pray in the spirit on all occasions with all kinds of prayers and requests."

"I say unto you my children, my chosen vessels, be brave and bold in the spirit of God and the spirit of truth. In these last days, I will draw all men unto myself from the four corners of the earth. My word is sharp and piercing like the two edged sword. When all else on earth is crushed, demolished, destroyed, my word shall stand. The devil cannot reach me. I will triumph over Satan and all his millions of demonic spirits. I am the great and mighty one you all sing, pray and worship. I am Jehovah. I am the root of Jesse! Let all thy kingdoms, palaces, and wealthy mansions upon the earth fall and crumble."

"All will shake and tremble at the sound of my voice. They will know that I am El Shaddai, mighty conquering warrior. Everyone will bow before my feet or die, I tell you this day. I, King Jesus, have had enough of all this false god worship on planet earth. Deny Satan and voodoo, witchcraft, Hinduism, Buddhism, Islam, and animal worship. Deny the worship of material items and yourself. Do not worship yourself as though you were a god. All is very sinful! All is idolatry. You will not enter the gates of heaven unless you acknowledge that I, Jesus Christ am your Lord, Savior, messiah, and Lord of your life. I am the only true God to worship and glorify. Repent of your sins and receive my mercy and loving kindness. Otherwise you will face all eternity burning in the flames and fiery pits of hell! My name is King Jesus, ruler and master of the universe. I have spoken and declared all these things today."

LOVE YOUR CREATOR

"My dear children upon planet earth, when will you make the choice to love your creator? God the father, yahweh and his only begotten son, Jesus, are the one in the same. They are forever trying to reach out to you, to shower you with many blessings and graces from above. When are you going to open your arms and accept all that God the father and his holy, anointed son, Jesus, have for you? They love you each beyond measure. God the father gave his only begotten son, Jesus, for the sins of the whole world so that all could enter the gates of heaven, after receiving and accepting their salvation, which is from Jesus Christ. Your savior, Jesus, was crucified on a wooden cross long ago for the sins of all humanity."

"When will you take your blinders off and see all the beauty of the earth? The sun, moon, stars, light, warmth, birds, mountains, lakes, seas, fish, animals, sports, music, art and children are all for your love and enjoyment. Jesus loves you more than you could ever imagine. He is your rock of salvation. He is a great treasure to behold. Don't let Jesus, your love, peace, and joy slip away from you. Won't you please bow and honor, praise, love and worship your creator? Jesus is your master, your abba father, and your best friend. Sing praises to his holy name. Worship and adore him. He is the mighty, victorious king of glory. He comes to reign in your heart. He wants to give you his unfailing love, peace, compassion, mercy, forgiveness, and loving kindness today. He holds back his wrath a little longer. Choose heaven and eternity with your maker and savior, Jesus Christ, or spend all eternity in the fiery pits of hell with Satan and all the millions of demons. Choose life with Jesus Christ. I beg you! Time is running out for you and your soul!"

Ringing of the Bells

"The ringing of the bells is in recognition of who I am, my greatness, my divine love, and my divine mercy for all mankind to receive. Ring the bells upon the earth for all generations to come to my holy and anointed presence."

"Let the bells ring throughout all the earth to show my love, my adoration to those who serve and honor me. Let bells ring throughout the heavens and the earth to show and declare my greatness, my glory, my abiding peace, care, and concern for all human life. Let not your hearts be troubled, dear children, for I am with you always till the end of all time. Accept my divine mercy as a bridge and a way to the arms of the father who abides in heaven. Ring the bells of your heart for my divine mercy and love to fill you to over flowing. Let your heart ring out a bell of freedom and love all peoples of all nations, races, and religions upon the earth. The bell is a symbol of this freedom, hope, abiding love, never ending I have for each of my children on earth. Carry this bell of love, peace and hope within your heart always and let it ring often. The sound of the bell ringing will echo and grow louder, penetrate the earth, sky and heavens and reach the very throne room of God the father. This is the choir bells I wish to see ringing upon the earth and in the churches. The bells of love for me, Jesus, your Christ, ringing with all the love within your heart for me and for all mankind. Let the bells ring out with all the love of the world for me and others. I wish to extend to each of you who love, worship, and serve me, my divine mercy and I wish to fill you with grace over flowing. Come to me at the foot of the cross and call upon me in your hour of need. Call out my name when you are sick. I will bestow my blessing and graces upon you my loving children."

"Jesus is a burning flame that can be ignited in the hearts of people who will worship him alone and no other god. I am an all-consuming fire. I will have no false gods before me. All will perish at the touch of my flame. I will consume all that is not adoring or honoring me, Jesus Christ. I am the only way to the father who sits on the throne in heaven. There is no other god to pray to, bow down to, or worship. Worship me alone I tell you. Surely a day is coming when the earth will be covered with brimstone, fire, flames, blood, and destruction. All will see who is the true God."

"I am the bread of life. Eat of me and you will live forever. Ignore me, spit upon me and you will face the flames of hell for all eternity. The choice is yours. Come, I say to all of you, before it is too late. Come and follow me. Pick up your cross and call out my name, Jesus, Jeshua, messiah, Jehovah. I am the good shepherd. You are all my sheep from the four corners of the earth. Time is short. I am the light of the world. Carry the flame of my light to all people of all nations before it is too late."

Baptism in Jordan River, Israel

Garden of Gethsemane, Israel

Jesus is the Good Shepherd

"Jesus, the good shepherd, is always abiding in the field. Look at me as I wear a cloak and hold a precious lamb. That could be each one of you my dear children. I long to hold you close to me and take good care of you. I don't want any harm to come to you. I created you all in my image. Humble yourselves before the sight of the Lord, your savior. Give me your love, praise, worship and adoration. Exalt my holy name, Jeshua, messiah, the son of the living God. There will come a day my children when you will regret that you would not listen to me or the messages and warnings. Then it will be too late. Change the direction of your life. Repent of your sins and come to the foot of the cross. I am waiting to show you mercy, forgiveness, love, peace, and joy. Hurry, time is running out."

King Jesus Will Reign on the Throne

"The love of Jesus reigns in the hearts of all his precious children upon the earth. Candles will light the path that will lead you to the throne room of the most, high God, and of his kingdom there will be no end. He is Jehovah Jirah, Jehovah Nissi. He is the Lord that healeth thee. By his stripes you shall be healed. All you who are weary, lost, confused, abandoned, abused, unwanted, lift up your eyes toward heaven and receive your miracle healing today. It may be a spiritual healing, an awakening, emotional healing, or a physical healing. All people and children are precious and special in the eyes of God. He places his countenance heavenly sphere around us. We are his chosen people. We are a loyal priesthood. He wishes for us to live and function within this heavenly realm atmosphere that is around us. We are enveloped in this sphere. Jesus dwells in the midst of our presence. He is a powerful, majestic, glorified sight to behold. He is our maker, our creator. Jesus holds all things and all people in the palm of his hand. Reach out and touch your king, your messiah, and your savior. He is the king of glory and the Lord of Lords forever. His name shall stand above all names in heaven and upon earth. Come and commune at the banquet table with the lamb of glory. He is the lamb that was slain for the sins of the whole world. Walk in the light of Jesus, your savior. He is the good shepherd. He wishes to lead you on a path of holiness. He is your peace and joy. Be purified by the blood of the lamb. Seek his face in the morning, noontime and evening. He is the peace and joy that surpasses all understanding. Surrender your life and all your earthly possessions to your Lord and God. Make a decision to follow the good shepherd today. His path leads into the kingdom of God for all eternity."

Enter and Walk Through the Gate

The kingdom of God is at hand. All you need to do is walk through the gate and eternal glory with the King of Kings and Lord of Lords. Jesus is the gate which you must pass through to enter the kingdom of God. Jesus is our master and ruler. He holds the key to our salvation. He will turn the key and unlock the gate to the kingdom of God. Open the gate, the very heart of Jesus, your messiah and savior. Be prepared to enter eternity with the King of Kings and Lord of Lords. He will adorn you with a crown of glory, and a fine garment, a robe to wear. You will receive riches, treasures to behold, a mansion in the sky, gemstones and many wealthy treasures and surprises. Your greatest reward will be to dine and have supper, communion with the great I am, the almighty who is the very bread of life itself.

Now is the time to rekindle the love you used to have for Jesus, the holy, anointed one. Come to the foot of the cross and repent of all your sins and wrong doings. Let Jesus give you a new heart filled with a new energy and a new spirit. This way you will receive a fresh anointing and a refreshing of the holy spirit within you. Receive a fresh refilling of the Spirit of God. It is yours for the taking.

Jesus says arise and step forward to receive all he has for you. Now is the time to turn the key, walk through the gate, which is Jesus, and enter the kingdom of almighty God for all eternity.

LET THE VEIL DOWN

Now is the time to enter into the very presence of God almighty, your everlasting father, your redeemer. Enter the throne room of the King of Kings and Lord of Lords. His name is King Jesus, abba father, messiah, redeemer, savior, the good shepherd, and Jehovah. He is the one worthy to receive all of your praise and worship. There is none like him in heaven or upon the earth. Crown him the king of glory. Let his light shine among all men. He is worthy to be praised and lifted up! He deserves all the glory, honor, and adoration that is due him. His name stands above all names. He is the spirit of the living God. He shall reign on his throne for all eternity. Let his glory shine upon all mankind and his holy light will penetrate the hearts of men in all nations.

His name is love. His name speaks peace. Let his glorious light surround you and fill you to over flowing with his shekeana glory. Jesus is your peace; the peace that surpasses all understanding. Receive that peace, love, and joy into your heart today. Become immersed in the holy light of Jesus and saturated with the all-powerful glory and majesty of the living God, the bread of life for all generations. Receive today all that your savior wishes to bestow upon you. Let his name be written upon your forehead for all eternity; the name which is above every name, Jesus. Jesus, how sweet the sound that saved a wretch like me. I once was lost, but now am found, was blind, but now I see.

Come and receive your salvation today and be set free from the chains that bind you. Let the veil down and surrender your heart, mind, body, soul, and all your earthly possessions to the king of glory. Salvation is yours to take freely and joyfully! Receive it today in Jesus' name.

Jesus, Victorious Warrior Waits for You

Jesus is the king of glory, now and forever, halleluiah! Let his light shine throughout all the earth. Let us clear away all the blindness and darkness. Let it pierce the enemy and may King Jesus, the victor of the spoils, make a joyful noise. Plant your feet on the solid ground of Christ. Do not step into the sinking sand. Stand firm on the solid rock of Christ and be a mighty witness for the king of glory. March forward in the king's army to the four corners of the earth with King Jesus. A glorious victory will be coming soon for the whole world to see. He is the king of victory! The mighty, victorious warrior!

He is the lifter of your head. Stand firm in the love of Jesus, your creator and savior. Do not march backwards. Go forward into new territory and see what the Lord has planned for you. Something wonderful! Something good! Surrender your heart and soul to King Jesus and he will be your gate, the door by which you will enter heaven for all eternity. Soar like an eagle and grab onto the hand of Jesus, the good shepherd, and let him lead you on a new path. All will be well with your soul.

For every mountain climbed is a great achievement in God's eyes. Start a new life, a new adventure, a new path. Now is the time to step forward and see what King Jesus has planned for you. Be excited, be happy. Good things are going to come to you, God's good and faithful servant; many blessings, graces, and happiness and desires of your heart. To God be all the glory! "I love you, sweet children of God."

Karen at Armageddon

Jesus is Your Healing Stream

Let not your heart be troubled. Jesus loves you and calls out to you in the quiet place of your heart. He is your healing stream. Come and step into the holy presence of Jesus, your savior. Step into the water. Be made whole today. Be forgiven, be set free. Let the chains be lifted. Come bathe in the waters of forgiveness and mercy. Jesus is waiting for you. He yearns to commune with and share his life with you. He wishes to heal and comfort you. He wants to love you and guide you on a path of holiness. He is the good shepherd. You are all his sheep. Come unto him. He will turn your sorrow into joy and your crying into dancing. Jesus is your healer.

Jesus Manifests His Glory

Jesus wishes to manifest his glory, love, and peace to you in a very real way. He gave you himself on the cross, in the Eucharist, in the presence of his holy spirit. Jesus is alive. He is the bread of life for all his children. He wishes to unlock your heart. Accept his unconditional love which he freely gives to you. Open your heart and let the king of glory enter. He wishes to fill you with love, blessings, graces over flowing. Always give thanks and adoration to your father in heaven and his son, Jesus Christ.

Many of you shall receive gifts of the holy spirit such as dreams, visions, words of knowledge, healing ministry, gifts of composing music, writing songs, singing, prophesying, and speaking and interpreting in tongues. His arms are extended for your embrace. Jesus is an all-consuming fire. He wishes for his flame to burn brightly in the heart of all his precious children. Give Jesus all the love, honor, and respect that is due him. He is alpha and omega; the beginning and end of all things. Let this be his finest hour. Let the world see his glory. Put all your burdens in the hands of your Lord and savior. Jesus freely accepted the crucifixion to set each of us free. Praise God! Thank you for Good Friday and Easter Sunday. After death, came the glorious resurrection of the lamb that was slain for the sins of the world. The chains were broken.

Death was defeated. He has risen. Halleluiah! He is truly the bread of life. Glorify the Lord today in the midst of your situations. Jesus will carry you through the storms. Now, you too, can live forever. The enemy has been defeated. You have been set free by the power of almighty God and washed clean by Jesus, the sacrificial lamb who is the king of glory, the victorious warrior.

Come and kneel before your maker, the King of Kings today. Arise, arise, in the name of Jesus. Be healed. Be cleansed. Be saved. Be set free. Let Jesus be glorified through you.

Amen.

ADDITIONAL THOUGHTS

"The light of Christ is for all on planet earth! Step into the light of me, Jesus Christ, and I will make your dreams come true. I am the light of the nations of the world. Come all people of all nations, tribes, races and tongues. Let me shed my light of glory upon all people this day. I wish to penetrate my light and my heat throughout all mankind. I carry the word of God. I come to rescue and save my beloved people. All will clam, peaceful, joyful, and happy when you come into the presence of my great and holy light. All will bow beneath my feet. All will recognize me as the messiah, the savior of the world. At my sight, every knee shall bow. All will exalt my holy name, Jehovah, Jesus Christ, the King of Kings and Lord of Lords. I am the Christ, the son of the living God, and my kingdom shall have no end. For I am alpha and omega; the beginning and end of all things. I am the flame that lights the whole world. I am the greatest flame, the hottest fire you could ever imagine. My glory and majesty shine across the heavens and the earth."

"Jesus is the good shepherd. He is always abiding in the field. Jesus wears a cloak and holds a precious lamb. He longs to hold you close to him. He wants to take care of you. Humble yourselves before the sight of the Lord, your savior. Give him your praise, worship and adoration. Bow before the foot of the cross and repent of your sins. Jesus will show you mercy, kindness, and forgiveness. He wishes to change your heart and capture it for himself. He is the good shepherd. He wants to set you free today and wipe every tear from your eyes."

"Step into the healing stream, the living waters of Christ's loving kindness today and receive salvation and the right to enter eternal glory; heaven with the King of Kings and Lord of Lords forever."

"Amen."

"For thine is the kingdom and the power and the glory forever and ever, Amen!"